SIMONE BILES

BY MATT SCHEFF

SportsZone

An Imprint of Abdo Publishing
abdopublishing.com

abdopublishing.com

Published by Abdo Publishing, a division of ABDO, PO Box 398166, Minneapolis, Minnesota 55439. Copyright © 2017 by Abdo Consulting Group, Inc. International copyrights reserved in all countries. No part of this book may be reproduced in any form without written permission from the publisher. SportsZone™ is a trademark and logo of Abdo Publishing.

Printed in the United States of America, North Mankato, Minnesota
102016
012017

Cover Photo: Kyodo/AP Images
Interior Photos: Rebecca Blackwell/AP Images, 4-5; Dmitri Lovetsky/AP Images, 6; Daniel Ramalho/Rex Features/AP Images, 7; Mike Blake/Reuters/Newscom, 8-9; Shutterstock Images, 10; Matthias Schrader/AP Images, 11, 20-21; Richard Ulreich/ZumaPress/Newscom, 12-13; David Drufke/ZumaPress/Newscom, 14-15; Elise Amendola/AP Images, 16-17; Andy Wong/AP Images, 18, 19; Amy Sanderson/Cal Sport Media/AP Images, 22-23; IBL/Rex Features/AP Images, 24; Michael Goulding/ZumaPress/Newscom, 25; Kyodo/AP Images, 26; Matt Dunham/AP Images, 27; Lukas Schulze/picture-alliance/dpa/AP Images, 28-29

Editor: Chrös McDougall
Series Designer: Jake Nordby

Publisher's Cataloging-in-Publication Data

Names: Scheff, Matt, author.
Title: Simone Biles / by Matt Scheff.
Description: Minneapolis, MN : Abdo Publishing, 2017. | Series: Olympic stars | Includes bibliographical references and index.
Identifiers: LCCN 2016951769 | ISBN 9781680785579 (lib. bdg.) | ISBN 9781680785852 (ebook)
Subjects: LCSH: Biles, Simone, 1997- --Juvenile literature. | Women gymnasts-- United States--Biography--Juvenile literature. | Women Olympic athletes-- United States--Biography--Juvenile literature. | Olympic Games (31st : 2016: Rio de Janeiro, Brazil)
Classification: DDC 794.44/092 [B]--dc23
LC record available at http://lccn.loc.gov/2016951769

CONTENTS

Simone Biles performs on the balance beam in the all-around finals at the 2016 Olympics.

OLYMPIC GOLD

US gymnast Simone Biles had work to do. The individual all-around competition at the 2016 Olympic Games was half over, and Biles trailed Russia's Aliya Mustafina. Then Biles wobbled on the balance beam. It was a situation nobody expected for Biles. She was the three-time defending world champion. Many assumed she would cruise to a gold medal.

But then Mustafina struggled even more on beam. Biles took over first place. Only the floor exercise remained.

Biles was nearly flawless on the floor. The 19-year-old opened with a full-twisting double layout. It was the beginning of a series of dizzying flips and spins. Each tumbling pass was more impressive than the one that came before it. Ninety seconds later, there was no doubt. Biles was the winner.

The tears came as she realized that she had achieved her dream. "Every emotion hit me at once so I was just kind of a train wreck," she said. But Biles had no time to rest. More Olympic gold would soon follow.

Biles, *left*, and US teammate Aly Raisman celebrate after Biles won gold and Raisman won silver in the Olympic all-around final.

Biles shows off her powerful tumbling on the floor exercise in the 2016 Olympic all-around finals.

FAST FACT
Biles won the all-around gold medal by 2.1 points. It was the largest margin of victory in the Olympics since new scoring went into effect in 2008.

TOUGH BEGINNINGS

Simone Arianne Biles was born on March 14, 1997, in Columbus, Ohio. Life started out tough for Simone. Her mother, Shanon, struggled with drug addiction. When Simone was three years old, Sharon gave up Simone and her three siblings. Simone's grandfather and his wife, Ronald and Nellie Biles, adopted Simone in 2003. They also adopted her younger sister, Adria.

9

From left, Ron, Nellie, and Adria Biles cheer on Simone at the 2016 Olympics.

Simone and her sister moved to an area directly outside of Houston, Texas. When Simone was six years old, she visited a gymnastics center. The trip changed her life. Simone watched the gymnasts doing flips and twists. She signed up and began her training. Simone's athletic ability made her a natural gymnast. Soon after, she began working with a young coach named Aimee Boorman. They proved to be a perfect match.

Simone and her sister moved to the Houston, Texas, area in 2003.

Simone and coach Aimee Boorman, *left*, stayed together through the 2016 Olympics.

Simone competes in the junior division at the 2012 US championships.

Simone had talent. But early on, she did not look like the world's best gymnast. Some observers said she lacked flexibility. In 2012 Biles started homeschooling. That gave her more time for training. The extra work paid off. By 2013, at age 16, Biles was ready to step up to the senior level. She was about to take on the best gymnasts in the world.

Biles perfects her form before the 2013 US Classic.

ROAD TO THE TOP

One of Simone Biles's first senior events was the 2013 US Classic. It was a disaster. She fell in each of her first three events. Her performance was so bad that her coach pulled her from the competition.

"Nothing was really going right," Biles explained later. "I guess I just wasn't in a very good mental place."

Biles worked to improve her focus. Less than a month later, she won the US all-around title. Fans were amazed by her difficult routines. Her power allowed her to do things that few other gymnasts could even try. Her skills were on display six weeks later at the 2013 World Championships. Biles won the all-around title by almost a full point.

Biles showed improved consistency at the 2013 US championships.

Biles lights up the floor exercise at the 2014 World Championships.

FAST FACT
Biles is scared of insects. At the 2014 World Championships, she darted off the podium when she saw a bee in her flowers!

Biles kept winning and winning—and winning. Many gymnasts excel on one or two apparatuses while struggling in others. But Biles was among the world's best in all four. She won world titles in floor exercise and balance beam. Her vault and uneven bars performances were among the best in the world, too. That versatility made her unstoppable in the all-around event. She was winning every one she entered. And the scores were not even close to those of her competitors.

Biles, *center*, shows off her all-around gold medal at the 2014 World Championships.

Biles performs on the balance beam at the 2015 World Championships.

Biles won all-around gold again at the 2015 Worlds. This time she beat her teammate and the reigning Olympic champ, Gabby Douglas. Biles totaled four gold medals and one bronze at the 2015 Worlds. It gave her a career total of 14 medals. That is the most in the history of women's gymnastics. She was so much better than everyone else that her teammates joked they were competing for second place.

Biles demonstrates excellent form on the balance beam at the 2016 US Olympic Team Trials.

GLOBAL STAR

Simone Biles was the best in the world by a wide margin. Just one thing remained: Olympic glory. Gymnastics is one of the most popular Olympic sports. Millions of people watch it on television.

The pressure was on. But Biles did not seem to notice. She cruised through the US Olympic Team Trials. No one came close to her performance. In August, she boarded a plane with her teammates. It was on to Rio de Janeiro, Brazil, for the Olympics.

FAST FACT

At the 2016 US championships, Biles landed a vault that scored a nearly perfect 9.9 on execution. The best possible execution score is 10. With a 6.3 difficulty score, her final score was 16.2.

Biles had one of the most difficult vaults at the Olympics.

FAST FACT

The "Final Five" nickname had two meanings. The 2016 squad was the last one put together by legendary coach Martha Karolyi. They were also the final five-person US women's team. Beginning in 2020 Olympic teams will have only four gymnasts.

Team USA was favored to win gold in Rio. And Biles was favored to star individually. She was a heavy favorite in the all-around. Experts predicted she could win as many as three more Olympic gold medals, too.

Biles and Team USA lived up to the hype. The US teammates called themselves the "Final Five." They began by winning team gold with a score of 184.897. Second-place Russia was more than eight points behind!

The "Final Five" celebrate their win.

FAST FACT
Biles was chosen to carry the US flag in the closing ceremony of the 2016 Olympic Games.

Biles shows her power during the floor exercise finals at the Olympics.

Biles easily won the all-around. Then she turned her attention to the individual events. Biles scored gold in the vault and the floor exercise. Her only misstep of the Olympics came in the balance beam. She was penalized for putting her hands on the beam to steady herself. The mistake dropped her to third place.

Biles still finished the Olympics with five medals—four gold and one bronze.

Fellow athletes pose with Biles at the closing ceremony.

Many have already called Biles the greatest in the history of women's gymnastics. But Biles does not want to be compared with other great Olympians. She wants people to understand that she is one of a kind.

"I'm not the next Usain Bolt or Michael Phelps," Biles said of two other superstars at the 2016 Olympics. "I'm the first Simone Biles."

Biles stands on the podium as the national anthem is played after receiving one of her 2016 Olympic gold medals.

TIMELINE

1997
Simone Arianne Biles is born on March 14 in Columbus, Ohio.

2003
Simone and her younger sister Adria are adopted by their grandfather and his wife, Ronald and Nellie Biles.

2003
Biles visits a gymnastics center and begins her training.

2012
Biles begins homeschooling so that she can spend more time practicing in the gym.

2013
Biles makes her senior international debut.

2013
Biles wins the all-around at the 2013 World Championships. She also wins the floor exercise.

2014
Biles's family starts its own gym.

2014
Biles wins four gold medals, including the all-around, at the 2014 World Championships.

2015
Biles wins her third straight all-around gold at the World Championships. She is named Team USA Female Olympic Athlete of the Year.

2016
Biles dominates at the 2016 Olympics in Rio de Janeiro, Brazil, winning four gold medals and one bronze.

GLOSSARY

addiction
A dependence on a substance such as drugs or alcohol.

adopt
To legally take in somebody else's child as your own.

all-around
A gymnastics competition in which women compete in all four events.

apparatus
One of four pieces of equipment in women's gymnastics: balance beam, floor exercise, uneven bars, and vault.

execution
The ability to properly complete a gymnastics routine.

flexibility
The degree to which a person can bend and move her or his body.

homeschooling
When a student takes classes at home instead of going to a school.

margin
The difference between two things.

routine
A set performance by a gymnast in one event.

senior
An elite gymnast who is more than 15 years old.

trials
An event that determines which athletes move on to a higher level of competition.

tumbling pass
A series in which a gymnast connects multiple gymnastics elements, such as flips and handsprings.

INDEX

About the Author

Matt Scheff is an artist and author living in Alaska. He enjoys mountain climbing, deep-sea fishing, and curling up with his two Siberian huskies to watch sports.